DRUGS AND WHERE TO TURN

A drug problem can lead to feelings of isolation and loneliness.

DRUGS AND WHERE TO TURN

Bea O'Donnell Rawls
Gwen Johnson

THE ROSEN PUBLISHING GROUP, INC.
NEW YORK

Published in 1993 by The Rosen Publishing Group, Inc.
29 East 21st Street, New York, NY 10010

First Edition

Manufactured in the United States of America

Library of Congress Cataloging-in-Publication Data

Rawls, Bea O'Donnell
      Drugs and where to turn / Bea O'Donnell Rawls and Gwen Johnson.
         p.   cm. — (The Drug abuse prevention library)
      Includes bibliographical references and index.
      Summary: Uses a real life story to look at some myths and facts about drugs and alcohol, and suggests ways to help yourself with abuse difficulties. Lists hotlines and organizations that help.
         ISBN 0-8239-1466-6
         1. Drug abuse—Juvenile literature.
         2. Teenagers—Drug use—Juvenile literature.
         [1. Drug abuse. 2. Alcoholism.] I. Johnson, Gwen. II. Title. III. Series
      HV5809.5.R39   1993
      362.29'18—dc20   93-20287
                                          CIP
                                          AC

Contents

Some teens begin to drink because they think it will add fun
to their lives.

CHAPTER 1

Drugs and Alcohol—The Answer or the Problem?

I've been in jail five times. I spent two months in a mental institution when I was 19. Three states took away my driver's license before I was 21. I lost more jobs than I can remember. And it all started so innocently when I was in junior high.

From school I only had to cross the railroad tracks to get to Toni's Pizza, where we ate lunch. No one noticed when we bought cigarettes from the machine. It took only three minutes to get to the oak trees down the hill behind the school.

That became our daily routine. Eat pizza for lunch, buy cigarettes, and smoke them where the teachers couldn't see us. Then one day Bill brought a six-pack of beer.

Bill, Sandi, Beth, and Patti all popped the tops on their cans and began to drink. I

8 ripped the tab off mine, took one big gulp, and thought to myself, "Carla, if you drink this fast, you can have more than anyone else." And I did. They each had one beer. I had two, and without ever knowing it I was hooked for life.

It was great. With two beers I became the center of our little party. I was with three of the most popular girls in school, and I was in the spotlight. That had never happened before.

Until good old Bill brought that beer, I was on the outskirts of the "in" crowd. I played first chair clarinet, got average grades in school, but always felt like I didn't fit. I sweat like crazy when popular kids talked to me. I never knew what to say.

But beer changed everything. Parties were fun, and I thought, "I want more of this." For the first time in my life I felt whole and equal to everyone else. I knew I was going to do this again. It felt great.

By the time I was in high school, I was the one who set up the parties. We spent the first few days of the week remembering the weekend fun. Thursday and Friday were for planning the weekend parties.

I loved the excitement of living close to the edge. We had to sneak around to figure *out how to get the stuff without getting caught. This was much better than being just plain, boring Carla.*

There were a lot of changes in me, but they were exciting changes. It wasn't long until I had new friends who liked to party as much as I did. I dropped the old friends who were like the old me—average and dull. I quit band, started using lots of makeup to be more like my new friends, and quit worrying about grades.

I remember thinking, "How can something feel so good if it's so bad?" Somebody must have been lying to me about drinking. Alcohol wasn't a problem. It was the answer to my problem.

Carla

Carla is a real person, and so are most of the details of her story. Names and facts have been changed to protect her privacy.

She may sound like someone you know. Her story is typical of what happens when drugs and alcohol find their way into someone's life. Carla is willing to tell it now because she knows that most people don't understand how it is from a user's point of view. She regrets not having had the facts when she was using.

10 | *Something's Going On in Your Life*

You had a reason to pick this book to read. Either you have an assignment to do on drugs and alcohol, or you're worried about drugs and alcohol in someone's life. Maybe your own.

When you're scared or worried, you look for answers to tough questions. It's easy for someone to tell you, "Just say no." The truth is it can be very, very hard to sort out the facts about drugs and alcohol.

Younger people often become addicted to nicotine faster than adults.

Looking at Carla's story, she didn't know the facts behind the myths about drugs and alcohol, and she got caught in their trap. She couldn't see why everyone said they were a problem. To her, they were the answer to her problems. She thought they made life more exciting and interesting. **MYTH ONE: Only old people, bad people, or bums become addicts and alcoholics.** Carla's road to addiction began when she drank those very first two beers. She didn't intend to become an alcoholic, but it happened. She was caught in the myth about the kinds of people who are alcoholics and drug addicts. She didn't fit the stereotype. She lived in a nice house and wore decent clothes. She was a girl and she was a kid. She wasn't the picture of someone down and out. Carla believed the myth.

Substance abuse exists everywhere. Drugs and alcohol don't make an age or an address check. Chemical dependency crosses all age and social groups. Doctors, truck drivers, teachers, parents, derelicts, teenagers, and even young children can become tangled in the web of drugs and alcohol. No one is completely safe from its meshes.

12 | **MYTH TWO: It takes a long time to become addicted.**
Sometimes it does, but sometimes it doesn't. How quickly a person becomes addicted depends on body chemistry. Age can also be important. Evidence suggests that young people become addicted much faster than older people.

There is no absolute way for people to know ahead of time if their chemistry is the kind that makes them easy victims of drugs and alcohol. Some people can use alcohol moderately all their lives and not become addicted. Others take the first step toward addiction the first time they use.

MYTH THREE: Addiction is all in your head.
Alcoholism is a disease. Like some other diseases, such as diabetes, alcoholism can run in families. Carla's grandfather was an alcoholic, and that increased the chance that she could become an alcoholic.

Not everyone who has an alcoholic relative will become an alcoholic. Even one alcoholic in your family makes drinking and using drugs very, very risky. The danger increases with the number of family members who are substance abusers. That includes aunts, uncles, cousins, and grandparents.

MYTH FOUR: It can't happen to me.

No one goes to the school counselor and says, "I want to be an alcoholic when I grow up." People don't become addicted on purpose. They use their drug of choice to feel better about themselves, to fit in with their friends, or to have a little fun. The risks of addiction are not evident in the beginning because alcohol and drugs seem to make life better.

Many diabetes-prone people never realize that the sugar-coated breakfast cereals they eat when they are young could lead to diabetes when they are older. They eat them and believe all the commercial messages that claim, "Sugar gives you energy." It's true, sugar gives a burst of quick energy, but it doesn't last. Alcohol and drugs make you feel as if you can be somebody, but that doesn't last either.

That's what happened to Carla. She thought she was having more fun and was the center of attention when she was drinking. She felt like everyone else.

Alcohol looked like the answer to her problem, and she wasn't about to believe what she'd been told—it was wrong and dangerous. She was convinced that was nothing but adult scare tactics—like the stories about the horrors of smoking.

14

Carla started smoking long before she started drinking. That was the first time she broke one of her own rules. When she was little, she told her dad he shouldn't smoke because it was bad for his health. But somewhere along the line she forgot her own rule.

She smoked her first cigarette when she was 11. Nothing horrible happened. So she smoked another. Before long smoking was a habit. She told herself that smoking was better than alcohol or drugs.

Carla didn't intend to drink either. She had seen what used to happen to her grandfather when he had too much to drink. He got mean. But those first two beers tasted so good. They made her feel wonderful. Again, nothing horrible happened. She broke another rule. It had to be another myth.

MYTH FIVE: Gateway drugs are safe.
The fact behind this myth is that common drugs often begin the process of breaking down behavior rules you set for yourself. These drugs are called *gateway drugs*.

Cigarettes (the drug is nicotine) are a gateway drug. Beginners say it's okay to smoke, but that's as far as it goes. No booze. No pills. Certainly no sex. Sex is much too dangerous.

Often beer and marijuana follow the
cigarette habit. Cigarette smokers rarely
stop smoking to take up marijuana or beer.
They keep adding to the drugs they already
use. They've just broken another rule.

Beer is easy to rationalize. *Everybody*
drinks beer, and it's easy to get. The fact is
that beer is NOT legal for people under 21
in most states. Hard liquor and harder
drugs are frequently the next broken rule.

Carla

By the time Carla was 17 she had broken
all of her own rules about drugs, alcohol,
and sex. She drank, smoked pot, popped
pills, and slept with people she barely
knew. She lied, stole, and cheated. Using
began to take its toll.

Carla was kicked out of school time and
time again. She became a dropout. Even
her family could take no more of her. At
17 they kicked her out too.

But Carla was having fun—she thought.
She was free, on her own.

What did her parents know? Or the old
friends she never saw anymore? They
were still in school, still in band, still
getting good grades, still boring.

How could something feel so good if it's
so bad?

CHAPTER 2

If I'm Having So Much Fun, Why Aren't I Laughing?

The arguments with my family got really intense just before they kicked me out. Mom never stopped nagging about staying out too late and drinking too much. She didn't like my new friends, and she hated the way I dressed. The last time I got kicked out of school she gave me $100 and told me if I wouldn't live by their rules, I could leave. I left.

It was tough applying for jobs. I kept thinking, "I can't do this. Working will cut into my party time." But I got a waitress job in a restaurant. It was the perfect place to make drug contacts. I was doing a lot of drugs by that time, and I bought them at work. Before long I was also selling, but I wasn't very good at it. I lost money doing it.

Every day was party time at my apartment, until I got kicked out of there too.

Alcohol does not solve any problems.

18

The funny part was they didn't evict me for loud parties. The problem was fruit flies. The apartment building was crawling with them, and the manager discovered they were coming out of my closet. The closet was full of empty beer cans I had dumped in there. The fruit flies moved in and multiplied.

No problem. I moved in with a friend. The best part of this arrangement was that his apartment was right across the street from my favorite bar. They accepted my false ID, so I was a regular there.

One night I was in there drinking when somebody gave me some lude [also known as Quaaludes]. *I washed them down with booze, stood up to go to the bathroom, and fell face first on the cement floor. I woke up in the emergency room. They pumped my stomach, and that was no fun. Lying in the hospital, I remember thinking, "I'd better not pop pills anymore—they're dangerous." I would just drink.*

I didn't want to go through that again. But I did—many times. It took more and more drugs and alcohol to maintain, and sometimes I overdosed. Having my stomach pumped was disgusting. The tube they shoved down my throat felt like a garden hose. It hurt.

My life was a mess, but it wasn't my fault. It was the people around me. The stupid manager at the restaurant fired me for missing work, so I cussed him out and partied a little harder. The guy I was living with threw me out because he thought I was a slob. I didn't need him anyway.

In my new place, I was in bed with some guy when my mother came in to tell me Grandad was in the hospital. She got mad when I couldn't remember the guy's name. How could I remember his name? I didn't know where I had met him.

It seemed as if everything in my life was falling apart. None of my plans ever worked out. I couldn't get a job. I tried junior college, but only lasted two days. I tried to get married, but even that fell through. The guy I had my eye on was straight, and he thought I was too. When he caught me smoking pot he was gone.

There were times when I was quite embarrassed by what I did when I was drunk or high. The mean things I said to my friends made me feel bad, but I never told them that. In a way, I felt like I had back in junior high—different and apart.

Life treated other people better. I blamed everybody, but especially my family. I

20 *thought if they hadn't thrown me out, maybe I wouldn't be in such deep trouble.*

This trouble was hard to understand. I had everything I wanted. I was on my own, nobody knew better how to have fun than I did, but I wasn't laughing.

I knew there was a problem, but I never dreamed it could be drugs or alcohol.

Reality Check

By now there is no question in your mind that Carla had a problem with drugs and

Admitting that you have a drug problem is the first step to overcoming it.

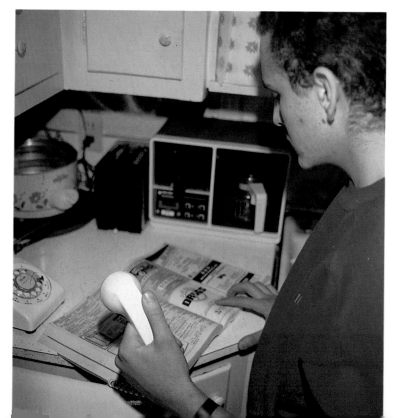

alcohol. She honestly never thought they could be the root of her troubles. They were the only part of her life that stayed the same. Everything else around her kept changing. Her friends, job, family connections, apartment, life-style, and values shifted from day to day. But drugs and alcohol were always there—like a best friend. How could that be the problem?

Many of the changes in Carla's life were unrecognized signals of substance abuse.

SIGNAL ONE: Attitude Differences

Carla's mother was convinced that Carla's trouble started with her new friends. Carla doesn't agree. She thinks her trouble started when she was kicked out of the house and on her own.

When Carla first started drinking she cared about what people thought of her. She hid what she was doing from her family because she knew they wouldn't approve. She partied hard with her new friends because she wanted to be a part of the group. Later, when she was deeper into addiction, she didn't care what anyone thought.

Carla's mom thought that if Carla would just straighten up everything would be okay. Carla thought life had dealt her a tough hand.

22   They were both right and they were both wrong. Carla's mother dealt with the disease by nagging. Nagging rarely changes anyone's attitude. Carla dealt with her disease by blaming her mother. She deliberately did things to make her mother mad. They set each other up.

Their attitudes about the issues meant something different to each of them. Their realities were different.

SIGNAL TWO: Preoccupation with Drugs and Alcohol

Substance abusers become preoccupied with finding ways to drink and use. They often base decisions about daily routines on how they affect the opportunity to drink or use. For example, to Carla a full-time job meant less time to party. The jobs Carla did get had to fit around using chemicals. Working was something to do between parties. She chose jobs where she could make drug contacts more easily.

SIGNAL THREE: Blackouts

Not remembering what happens when drinking or using drugs is a warning signal of a problem with chemicals. It is called a blackout. A whole block of time simply disappears. There is no memory of what happened, where you were, who you were with, or what you did. Carla couldn't

Loss of control over your life is a sure sign of a serious drug problem.

remember the party where she met the guy her mother found her with. It was a blank spot in her memory.

Users can walk, talk, eat, and dance but not remember it. It's a scary thought, but some even try to drive. Many times they deny having done something the next day because they have no memory of it.

SIGNAL FOUR: Loss of Control

People under the influence of drugs or alcohol often make decisions they wouldn't make if they were sober. Carla

24 | was not stupid. She knew that mixing drugs and alcohol was dangerous, but when she was drinking or using drugs her mind didn't compute the facts. She lost control and did whatever sounded good at the moment. That is why she ended up in the hospital so many times.

Reason and judgment are blocked by chemicals. They dull the ability to think straight. It is not a matter of making good or bad decisions. It's a matter of not being able to make healthy decisions. Carla was not a bad person who needed to be good. She was a sick person who needed to get well.

SIGNAL FIVE: Changed Values

Values are rules you make to live by. They are your personal code of what is okay to do and what is not. You learn the basis of them from your family.

Carla's rules were solid when she was little, but they changed as she used more and more substances. She didn't like smoking when she was a child, but she tried it anyway. She thought it was one way to be more like everyone else, even though not everyone in her class smoked. Drinking was also out because of her grandfather, but eventually she tried that too. Drugs were next. Then sex. She cheated on her friends. Each time she broke one of her rules, it was easier to break the next one.

When she was clean and sober, she didn't feel good about the changes in her rule book. She felt sleazy; she felt like a loser. So she used more drugs and alcohol to cover up those bad feelings. Drugs and alcohol helped her forget that she wasn't living what she believed in way down deep.

SIGNAL SIX: Not Caring

Not caring about much of anything is closely related to the change in values. Not caring often shows up in appearance. Guys sometimes develop a beer gut. They don't like being sloppy, but drinking is easier and more fun than staying sober and in shape. Girls often begin to use more and more makeup. Partly their senses become so dulled that they can't tell how much is enough. It takes more and more makeup to look as if they are wearing any.

Not caring about life comes into the picture too. Dreams and goals are set aside. It seems as if nothing matters and nobody cares. The major focus is on partying right now. Thinking about the responsibilities of growing up is too much to deal with. Life feels like the pits.

Family relationships may be altered or destroyed because of drug use.

When Carla said, "Life really sucks," she had slipped into the I-don't-care-anymore pitfall.

SIGNAL SEVEN: Complaints from Friends

It's bad enough to have parents nag about everything you do, but it's really a bummer when your friends start in on you too. They remind you of things you would rather forget. They complain about how you act and how you treat them. Sometimes they can't take your behavior anymore, and the friendship ends.

Carla's friend finally threw her out of the apartment because he couldn't stand living with a slob. He was tired of the messes she made but never cleaned up. He didn't want to bail her out of jail any-more, and he was sick of cleaning up the bathroom when she threw up. He said, "Enough," and she was out.

Carla got mad at him because he wasn't being a very good friend. She couldn't see what a pain *she* was.

SIGNAL EIGHT: Change of Friends

Friends make your world go around. It's hard to live without them. People choose each other as friends because they have something in common. Friends like the same things.

28

When old friends suddenly don't seem important anymore, it's time to take a look at why they don't. Someone is changing. Is it you or they? Are drugs and alcohol the main thing you have in common with your new friends?

If troubles seem to follow you and your new, exciting friends, it may be a signal for you to take a second look. Could your choice of friends be part of your problem? Is it easier to break your own rules when you're with them? Have you put yourself in a danger zone?

Those are tough questions to answer. Carla's friends changed very quickly when she started to drink and use. The new friends were more exciting, but she found them hard to count on. They dropped her when they didn't need her or got tired of her.

Carla didn't know that her choice of friends might be a signal of substance abuse. She didn't recognize the other signals of substance abuse in her life.

She knew something was wrong, but she didn't know what. It never occurred to her that drugs or alcohol could be the problem. The only thing she knew for sure was that she wasn't laughing very much anymore.

CHAPTER 3

Is There Someone to Talk To?

The day I woke up in a mental institution, I thought my life was over. The police picked me up on a bridge at 4:30 in the morning. The rivets and bolts looked like scorpions, and I was swatting at them with a broken beer bottle. They hauled me in, and a judge committed me on a mental hold. They had to be nuts if they thought I needed mental help.

Nothing ever scared me as much as being in there. Suddenly I had no control over anything. Someone else decided everything that happened to me. I couldn't even decide when to take a shower or brush my teeth. I felt totally helpless and more alone than I'd ever been in my life.

30

Every day a doctor came by to talk. I wasn't the least bit interested in what he had to say. One day he said, "Carla, I think you're an alcoholic."

*That was the dumbest thing I'd ever heard. Didn't he see me? Didn't he know where I was? I was 19 years old and confined to a mental institution, for God's sake. There were **really** sick people in there, and I wasn't one of them.*

I had no idea when I would get out or even whether I would get out. And he had the nerve to suggest I was an alcoholic? That guy wasn't playing with a full deck.

He kept talking about it, even though I guaranteed him there was not a chance in the world I had a problem with booze. It simply wasn't so.

After several days of this, he said he could get me a pass to go to an AA [Alcoholics Anonymous] meeting with him. Now I could get excited about that. If agreeing with him was my ticket out of there, I'd be an alcoholic or anything else he wanted.

The AA meeting was a gas. I learned how to play their game. I told them what they wanted to hear, and it worked. They released me after two of the most miserable months of my life.

These young people have taken the first courageous step toward recovery by joining this rehabilitation group in Queens, New York.

The constant need for drugs often leads to criminal acts.

I was clean and sober when I hit the streets, but it didn't last long. The first thing I did was find some booze. Five hours on the outside and I was drinking again.

The next three years are a blur. Most of it I don't remember. I have pictures of myself with people I don't know in places I don't recognize. I found match books in my pockets and purse from bars in states I didn't remember going to.

32

I think I drifted across the United States, but I don't know where I went or whom I went with. The little I do remember is fuzzy.

Early one morning I woke up in a motel room on the West Coast with a man and a woman I'd never seen before. That was a jolt. Not only were they strangers, but so was the name of the town on the motel's welcome sign. I didn't even know what state we were in.

As I looked around the room, I heard the faint echo of something I had heard before: "Carla, I think you're an alcoholic." I couldn't remember where I had heard it.

Over and over, "Carla, you're an alcoholic." "An alcoholic." "Alcoholic. . . Alcoholic." I couldn't get that sentence out of my head.

Phone books are a wealth of information, and motel rooms always have one. I looked up the number of AA and called. A man answered and said he'd have someone come to get me in 15 minutes.

In less than 15 minutes, I left that motel room and the two people I was with. I never did find out who they were.

The people from AA got me dried out, and I started going to meetings again. My new friends helped me get a job and a place to live.

34

It wasn't easy those first few months. I felt as if I were hanging on to the side of the world with only my fingernails. But my AA friends were there to listen and help me get a stronger hold.

If only I had realized sooner how easy it was to find someone to talk to.

Risk Equals Opportunity

Ancient Chinese wisdom tells us, "Risk equals opportunity." Carla knew that instinctively. She was willing to risk being labeled an alcoholic to get out of the confines of the mental institution. But she didn't believe for a minute that alcohol was her problem.

Long before she was committed, she took risks. Each time she broke one of her rules, she took a risk. She thought the risks equaled more opportunities for fun. Carla faced the daily risks of accident, attack, overdose, AIDS, and pregnancy. But she thought those things only happened to other people.

The most important risk in Carla's life was too scary to take. She was afraid to tell someone about the mess she was in. She didn't know what would result. It might not be the kind of opportunity she wanted.

When Carla was still in high school, she
had tried to talk to her grandmother about
what was going on in her life. She knew
something was wrong, but she wasn't clear
about what it was. When she tried to tell
her grandmother about the confusion she
felt, she was too vague. Her grandmother
didn't understand the message. Carla didn't
feel safe enough to say she was doing drugs
and drinking regularly. Her family wouldn't
approve, and she knew it.

Horrible images ricocheted in her head
about what would happen if her family
found out. She imagined that they would
send her to a juvenile home, or take her
car away, or ground her until she was 92.
Maybe they would even make her see a
shrink!

Carla did what so many people do. She
stumbled along alone. She didn't know
how to identify the right person to reach
out to. She didn't know how to find
someone to be her personal cheerleader.

Finding the Right Cheerleader

Moving out of the familiar territory of
silence was scary. There is a very real
danger that the person you choose to talk
to won't understand. And you might be
right. People who don't rely on drugs and

36 alcohol sometimes *don't* understand how terrifying it can be to have those familiar "friends"—drugs and alcohol—taken away. That was Carla's fear when she tried to talk to her grandmother. She was sure her family would give her a lecture about using and drinking.

At first Carla's need was to talk to someone. That's all—just talk. She ached to have someone she trusted who would listen. That's all—just listen. Not to judge or to moralize or to tell her what's right and what's wrong. Just to listen.

When drugs take control over your life, the situation seems hopeless.

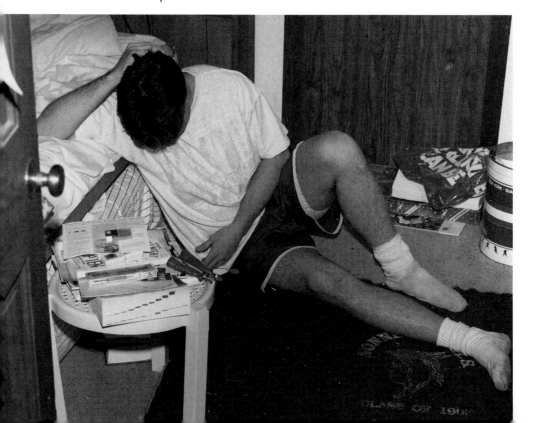

But how does a person find that special friend—a cheerleader who will just listen? Where do you look? How do you take that first risky step?

Taking the First Step

It is usually fear that holds people back from talking about drugs and alcohol. The first step involves identifying the fear.

Ask yourself the following questions:

1. Am I afraid of what people will think? Drug addiction and alcoholism are both diseases. Both of these diseases will get progressively worse unless treated. If left untreated, the victim of alcoholism or drug addiction will eventually die of the disease or a related complication.

If Carla's life had been in danger from a disease such as diabetes, people would have fussed over her, been sympathetic and supportive.

Friends who recognize that someone is suffering from the disease of alcoholism or drug addiction are sympathetic and supportive. But if they don't accept addiction as a disease, they may think the user is just wild and inconsiderate.

Regardless of what people think, the user *must get help as soon as possible.* Treatment in the early stages of the disease increases the chance of recovery and will usually shorten the time in treatment.

There is no contest between recovering from a disease and what people think. Getting well wins.

2. Will people judge me?

People have opinions, and opinions are a kind of judgment. But judging isn't always bad. People often think judgments are negative. That is not always true; often a judgment can be a compliment.

Friends who know that addiction is a treatable disease will be impressed with the user who is wise enough to look for help.

Carla didn't discover that until she risked calling the phone number for AA.

3. Do I have to tell where I get the drugs and alcohol?

Talking to someone about what is going on in your life does not require ratting on friends or connections.

Carla found out when she reached out to AA for help that nobody really cared where she got her drugs and alcohol. Their only concern was that she become clean and sober. They didn't care about her connections. They wanted her to experience recovery as they had in their own lives.

There is a separation between law enforcement and getting help for a serious illness. If you are messing with an illegal substance, law-enforcement officials are interested in your source, but counselors are not. Each has a job to do, and each job is important. Talking to a friend, teacher, or counselor about getting help is about wellness, not punishment.

4. Will I get into trouble?
Can you identify what "trouble" is?

Answer this question with two more questions: (1) Will the mess I'm in get better if I don't get help? and (2) What can anyone actually do to me that's worse than what is already going on?

Making the Move
Once you've sorted out your fears, talking to someone is the next step.

There is an old saying: "When the student is ready, the teacher will appear." For the substance abuser it could be, "When the talker is ready, the listener will appear." The listener may be standing within arm's reach, so look around.

Special People
Special people, willing to listen, were all around Carla the same way they surround

40 most users. Family members are special people whom users often miss. Carla's grandmother loved her and wanted to help her, but Carla didn't risk telling her story clearly. She only hinted about what was on her mind. Her grandmother missed the message, and Carla missed a faithful, loving listener.

Grandparents are not the only family members available to be cheerleaders. Parents, stepparents, brothers, sisters, aunts, uncles, and cousins are all possible caring listeners for a user willing to take the risk.

School Connectors

The user who is still in school has a gold mine of possible listeners. Carla's band teacher was a good friend. She trusted him, but she didn't think to talk to him

Nearly everyone has a special teacher. An elementary teacher might be the one the user trusts most. It's okay to go back to your grade school. Teachers don't forget special people either.

Check with a counselor. Counselors are bound by the law to honor confidential conversations. They are in the business of helping people in trouble. Remember, there is nothing new. The counselors have heard it already. They will not pass judgment or call your parents. They will only encourage you to talk to them.

Most schools have a Student Assistance Program with a trained drug and alcohol counselor in charge. Your school may have a different name for the very same program. If you don't know where it is, ask around or look for posters on bulletin boards. It won't be hard to find.

Coaches, classroom teachers, special ed teachers, health nurses, custodians, secretaries, principals, and vice principals care about students and what happens to them. Look around for the one with whom you feel the most comfortable. Ask yourself if the person has proved to be trustworthy in other situations. If so, you may have found the right person at the right moment.

Community Organizations

Occasionally people prefer to talk to someone who is not as close as family members or people at school. For them, there's a wealth of good listeners in the community.

Think about the organizations or youth groups you belong to or know about. Boys and girls clubs, Scouts, religious youth

42 groups, and 4-H are organizations for young people. If you don't belong to one of these groups, you can go with a friend who is a member.

Look for a drug and alcohol treatment program in your community. Such programs have trained drug and alcohol counselors who lead teenagers in group sessions that talk about drug and alcohol problems.

Some treatment programs are tax-supported and cost little or nothing. The fee scale depends on a person's ability to pay. Other treatment facilities, however, are privately owned businesses and charge for their services. A user going to a drug and alcohol counselor is like a diabetic going to a medical doctor. Medical doctors charge for treatment, and so do drug and alcohol counselors.

Talking to a drug and alcohol counselor in a treatment program means that you are getting help from someone who works with substance abuse problems every day.

Support Groups

Carla found someone she could talk to in Alcoholics Anonymous. All she had to do was call and someone was there to listen. She could have called NA (Narcotics

A counselor or friend can help to set up a program for recovery.

44 Anonymous). She chose AA because it is more widely known. AA worked for her.

Two similar organizations are Alateen and Al-Anon.

Alateen is for young people who are NOT alcoholics but have a parent(s) who is. This group helps teens deal with the difficulties alcoholism dumps on families. An alcoholic teen should call AA, not Alateen.

Al-Anon is for adult family members of alcoholics. It provides the same kind of support for older family members that Alateen does for young people.

Finding Organizations to Contact

Carla used the telephone to find AA, her first cheerleader. The telephone can be a lifeline for someone in trouble with drugs and alcohol. Do as Carla did. Look up helping organizations in the phone book. They are listed in the yellow pages under headings such as Addiction, Alcohol, Drugs, or Crisis Intervention Counseling. Also look for the community service page number in the Table of Contents. On this page you will find listings for alcohol and drug abuse, counseling, and crisis numbers.

Helpline or Hotline

Call a local Helpline or Hotline for someone to talk to. These services have volunteers available 24 hours a day. The volunteers are trained to be good listeners. They do not do long-term counseling, and they can't come to get you if you're in trouble. They listen, offer suggestions, and provide direction for help. They can give you phone numbers of other helping organizations.

You can also call the National Drug Hotline. That number is: 1-800-622-HELP. These volunteers are also good listeners with experience in knowing what to suggest.

Treatment Centers

Treatment centers are another possible choice for someone to talk to. The telephone book lists the treatment centers in your community. Again, look in the yellow pages under headings such as Alcohol, Drugs, Addiction, or Counseling.

Bulletin Boards

Bulletin boards often have flyers about where to turn for help. Look for them in schools, libraries, grocery stores, teen nightclubs, churches, buses, subways,

46 | skating rinks, parks, restrooms, shopping malls, and theaters. Any place you find a bulletin board, you will probably find a number to call.

Posters

Posters commonly have information about where to go or whom to call for help or someone to talk to. Posters are in many public places.

Carla didn't realize there were so many people out there to talk to until she started to look around. She was surprised to discover that people were not only out there, but that they cared about helping her without passing judgment.

If you need to talk to someone, look around. Take a risk. There are lots of people who care.

CHAPTER 4

For Students Only

"Why me?" "Why me?" Carla asked herself that difficult question for several months after she had become clean and sober. The good life had been set up for her from the time she was little. Her family were ready to help her go to college, so education was no problem. She was intelligent, energetic, attractive, and healthy. All she had to do was to take advantage of the opportunities in front of her. But she blew it all for drugs and alcohol.

What went wrong? Why couldn't she party like other people who didn't become addicted? Was she different? Was it bad luck? Or an ugly joke?

Gradually Carla came to understand herself and see a pattern in the addictive process. She learned that understanding

47

"Why me?" was not as important as Carla's learning to accept herself as an alcoholic/addict. Eventually Carla figured out how to use her love for adventure and freedom to help her stay clean and sober.

Everyone enjoys adventure. People like being a little scared. They say, "I want to be me." Carla sang it long, loud, and strong. Each person holds a slightly different view of what is an adventure. For Carla it was being the center of a party. She was good at taking risks and living close to the edge. The risks she took for adventure and freedom were tangled in drugs and alcohol. She needed to learn how to make taking risks work for her, and she did.

Sobriety Is Not Easy

The decision to talk to someone about your problem is hard. The decision to stop using is hard. For a user, life without drugs and alcohol is scary. Life is scary. To the addict, sober risks are the hardest and scariest of all.

If you are reading this book because you want to change how drugs and alcohol affect your life, get ready for one of the toughest struggles you will ever have. But you can do it.

A life filled with constructive interests and activities will be
fulfilling and satisfying.

50

Taking a book about drugs and alcohol off the shelf is a big step toward changing the direction of your life. You have the power to choose between drugs and alcohol and a clean and sober life. It won't always be easy. But the rewards are great. Recovering addict/alcoholics will tell you how much better their lives are now. You can only know how great recovery is by discovering it yourself

Stages of Recovery

Substance abusers go through predictable stages in recovery. Carla did. Each stage is normal and to be expected, and each stage is scary and risky.

Denial

Before users decide to get help, they are usually in the early stage of recovery called denial. They insist that they don't have a problem, or they minimize how big the problem is. They think: "Others may have a problem, but I don't. I can handle it. Life is screwy, not me. Besides, I only party on weekends." Carla was in denial big time.

A user in denial probably won't read this or any other book on drugs and alcohol voluntarily. That person is not ready. A user in denial doesn't want to admit that there might be a problem.

Admitting is really hard. It's depressing to face the facts.

If you have friends or family you're worried about, gently encourage them to read this book or another one. Reading might get them to stage two in recovery.

Admitting

Stage two is admitting. Reaching out to talk to someone about what is wrong in your life is the first stage of admitting that you're in trouble. Talking to people, reading books like this one, noticing how drugs and alcohol play a part in other people's lives are all part of the early stages of recovery. To solve the problem, a user must then take action.

Carla's initial attempt to talk to her grandmother was the beginning of admitting that her life was out of control. That was when she began to doubt her choices.

If you see any of the many signals of substance abuse in your life, don't wait as long as Carla did. Find someone to talk to fast if you aren't laughing anymore.

Acceptance

Actively looking for and taking part in drug and alcohol treatment programs is stage three—acceptance. This is the beginning of reclaiming your life.

52   Working with skilled drug and alcohol counselors is the most effective way to find and maintain sobriety, but not the only one. Some people can kick their destructive habits alone. It's the hard way to do it. The risks of relapse are greater when a user tries to become clean and sober alone. A substance abuser needs an organized plan and a support team to help prevent relapse. The temptation to use doesn't go away without a fight. You can count on that.

    Carla accepted her problem with drugs and alcohol when she called AA. She found recovery because she had a support team through AA and a plan to prevent relapse.

Surrender

The fourth and final stage of recovery is surrender. Surrender is a combination of admitting there is a problem, accepting it, and then taking the necessary action to become clean and sober.

    Staying clean and sober is recovery. It goes on for the rest of your life. There is no magic time when the ordeal is over. Carla discovered that once an alcoholic, always an alcoholic. The goal is to be able to say, "I'm a *recovering* addict/alcoholic."

Getting involved with drug-free friends will be a positive step to a better future.

Carla

Telling you about what happened to me is hard. There's a part of me that doesn't want to admit what happened. I still worry about what people will think. Being accepted is as important to me now as it was in junior high. The difference is that now I'm not willing to pay the price I did then. The price I paid was my self-respect. I couldn't look anyone in the eye, and I didn't like what I saw in the mirror.

54

I don't celebrate my birthday anymore. But I do celebrate my clean and sober day. I celebrate it because my life didn't really begin until I took my last drink and stopped using drugs.

Last week I had a party. I have been clean and sober for five years. It hasn't been easy, but I'm alive. I don't think I would be if I hadn't stopped using. I learned that I could live without drugs and alcohol. Now I take my recovery one day at a time.

I've learned a lot these past five years. I learned that no matter what I did or what happened to me, someone else had it worse. My drug and alcohol counselor used to tell me that there's nothing new, nothing original. It's true. Someone somewhere has done worse things and had worse things happen.

Don't think you're alone. You can find people who understand no matter how bad your life is. Look around for someone to talk to. Someone has probably been next to you all along. As scary as it is, don't overlook your parents. If you're sincere about getting clean and sober, they will understand and help you. Parents can be the strongest support of all. If you go into treatment, they will have to know to help pay for it. It took a long time before I realized that my family were there for me all along. All I had to do was talk to them. Chances are your parents already suspect what the problem is. Mine did.

Regardless of whom you decide to talk to, be clear about what you are saying. First, I beat around the bush and no one understood me. I wish I had known that I could say I was scared. I didn't know it was okay for me to talk to them about drugs and alcohol. Is it hard to talk to parents? You bet it is—but only in the beginning.

If talking is too scary for starters, write a letter. I wish I had. Leave it where the person you want to talk to is sure to find it. Tape it to the bathroom mirror. Stick it on the refrigerator door. Leave it on the person's pillow. Write about how you feel. Be more honest than you have ever been in your life.

Give the person time to think about what you have said. The real conversation is easier after the ice is broken. It won't be easy, but will your life get any better without some help?

It was hard for me just being a teenager. The world is full of tough choices. I made a lot of unhealthy decisions about drugs and alcohol. But it's not too late for you to take a healthy path. It takes courage to change.

56 *Talking about your problem is the beginning of change. Dig deep. You're stronger than you think. I'm making it, and so can you.*

The most exciting thing I've learned is that being sober isn't dull or boring. Life is one big adventure. I have more freedom than I ever had as an alcoholic/addict. Life gets better every day. I feel connected and alive. I see life and live it.

Recovery takes time—lots of it. I use rewards to help maintain recovery. I promised myself a new car for five years of being clean and sober. I have a brand-new car now, and it costs less per month than I spent on drugs and alcohol. There are days when I wonder if it's all worth it. Then I go cruising in my shiny red car and I know that it is.

I missed most of my teenage years. I was too stoned to remember or enjoy them. I can't get them back, but maybe by telling you my story I can help you save yours.

I found out the hard way why I wasn't laughing anymore. Drugs and alcohol were not the answer to my problems. They were my problem.

Help List

Where to Call

There are many reasons why you might want to talk to someone about drugs and alcohol or other problems in your life. Most telephone books list numbers for organizations devoted to helping people in need. Many other problems may need attention. They may not be connected to substance abuse, but often they are.

The following organizations have people who will talk to you. They will not tell anyone what you say. They will tell you where you can go for more help.

If the number begins with 1-800, there is no charge. The other numbers do have a long-distance charge. DO NOT call a 1-900 number for help; trustworthy services do not use 1-900 numbers. But do call any other number listed even if it costs a few cents. A few minutes of long-distance charges are cheaper than a lifetime of illness.

Alateen

This is a support group for teenagers who have a family member who is an alcoholic. If there is no listing for Alateen, call the number for AA and ask if there is a nearby Alateen group.

58

AA (Alcoholics Anonymous)
Many have a 24-hour hotline number.
CA (Cocaine Anonymous)
> **1-213-559-5833**
Cocaine Baby Hotline
> **1-800-327-BABE** (in Illinois, Indiana, Kentucky, Michigan, Minnesota, Missouri, or Wisconsin.) **1-312-908-0867** (in other states.)
DA (Drugs Anonymous)
> **1-212-874-0700** (New York area)
Drug and Alcohol Hotline
> **1-800-252-6465**
National Council on Alcoholism and Drug Dependency
> **1-800-NCA-CALL, or**
> **1-800-622-2255**

Ethnic-Oriented Services
Calix Society
> **1-612-546-0544**
This Catholic society sponsors support groups for recovering alcoholics.
Indian Health Service (IHS)
Regional programs to help Native Americans and Alaskan Natives with drug and alcohol treatment.
> Alaska   1-907-257-1652
> Arizona   1-602-241-2170
> California 1-916-978-4191

Minnesota 1-218-751-7701
Montana   1-406-657-6944
New Mexico 1-505-552-6634
Oklahoma 1-405-231-5181
Oregon   1-503-221-4138
South Dakota 1-605-226-7456
Tennessee 1-615-736-5104   x 35

Institute on Black Chemical Abuse (IBCA)
   1-312-663-5780
Jewish Alcoholics, Chemically Dependent
Persons and Significant Others (JACS)
   1-212-473-4747
National Asian Pacific Families Against Abuse
   1-301-530-0945
National Coalition of Hispanic Health and
Human Services
   1-202-371-2100

Help Services for Related Problems
Child Help USA
   1-800-4-A-CHILD, or 1-800-422-4453
   A hotline for victims of child abuse.
Covenant House Nineline
   1-800-999-9999
Incest Survivors Anonymous
   1-213-428-5599
A hotline for victims of incest.
National Runaway Hotline
   1-800-231-6946
   1-800-392-3352 (Texas only)

Glossary

Explaining New Words

addict Person dependent on drugs or alcohol.

Al-Anon Organization of men and women whose primary purpose is to support family members of alcoholics.

Alateen Support fellowship for teenagers who have parents with drinking problems.

alcoholic Person who suffers from the disease of alcoholism. An alcoholic has lost the ability to control the use of alcoholic beverages.

Alcoholics Anonymous Organization of men and women whose primary goal is to stay sober and help others stay sober.

alcoholism Chronic, progressive, addictive disease.

blackout Inability to remember what happened when under the influence of drugs or alcohol.

connection A person or place where drugs or alcohol can be obtained.

dependency Having lost the ability to
control use of drugs and alcohol.
drug abuse Excessive use of a drug short
of dependence.
gateway drugs First drugs used.
Nicotine (tobacco in any form) is the
most common gateway drug.
genetic history Family medical history
from which you could inherit
characteristics.
Narcotics Anonymous A worldwide
organization of men and women
dedicated to remaining drug-free and
helping others become drug-free.
overdose Consumption of drugs or
alcohol to a level that endangers the
user's life.
Quaaludes Powerful chemical that acts
as a sedative; a "downer."
recovery Process of returning to a normal
life-style free of all chemicals.
student assistant program School-
sponsored program with counselors
available to help students become and
remain drug-free.
treatment Medical or nonmedical
techniques that help a substance abuser
become and remain clean and sober.

For Further Reading

Black, Claudia. *It Will Never Happen to Me.* New York: Ballantine, 1987.

Childress, Alice. *Hero Ain't Nothin' But a Sandwich.* Long Beach: Cornerstone, 1989.

Coffey, Wayne. *Straight Talk about Drinking: Teenagers Speak Out.* New York: New American-Dutton, 1988.

Edwards, Gabrielle I. *Coping with Drug Abuse,* rev. ed. New York: Rosen Publishing Group, 1990.

Edwards, Gabrielle I. *Drugs on Your Streets.* New York: Rosen Publishing Group, 1991.

McFarland, Rhoda. *Coping with Substance Abuse.* New York: Rosen Publishing Group, 1990.

Robertson, Nan. *Getting Better: Inside Alcoholics Anonymous.* New York: Fawcett, 1989.

Seixas, Judith S. *Drugs: What They Are, What They Do.* New York: William Morrow and Co., 1991.

Snyder, Anne. *My Name is Davy. I'm an Alcoholic.* New York: New American-Dutton, 1986.

Index

About the Authors

Bea O'Donnell Rawls is the Director of Outreach Programs for Rogue Community College. She was a high school counselor for nineteen years, advising students and families with chemical abuse problems. Ms. Rawls also taught secondary English, speech, and journalism for five years.

Gwen Johnson is the founder and executive director of Basics, Inc., a family-oriented substance-abuse treatment facility for adults and adolescents.

Her career includes directing student assistant programs for chemically dependent students and providing outpatient treatment for teenagers and for abusers with multiple addictions.

Photo Credits

Cover: Stuart Rabinowitz.
Page 31: © Stephen Ferry/Gamma-Liaison; p. 32: Wide World Photos. All other photos by Stuart Rabinowitz.

Design & Production: Blackbirch Graphics, Inc.